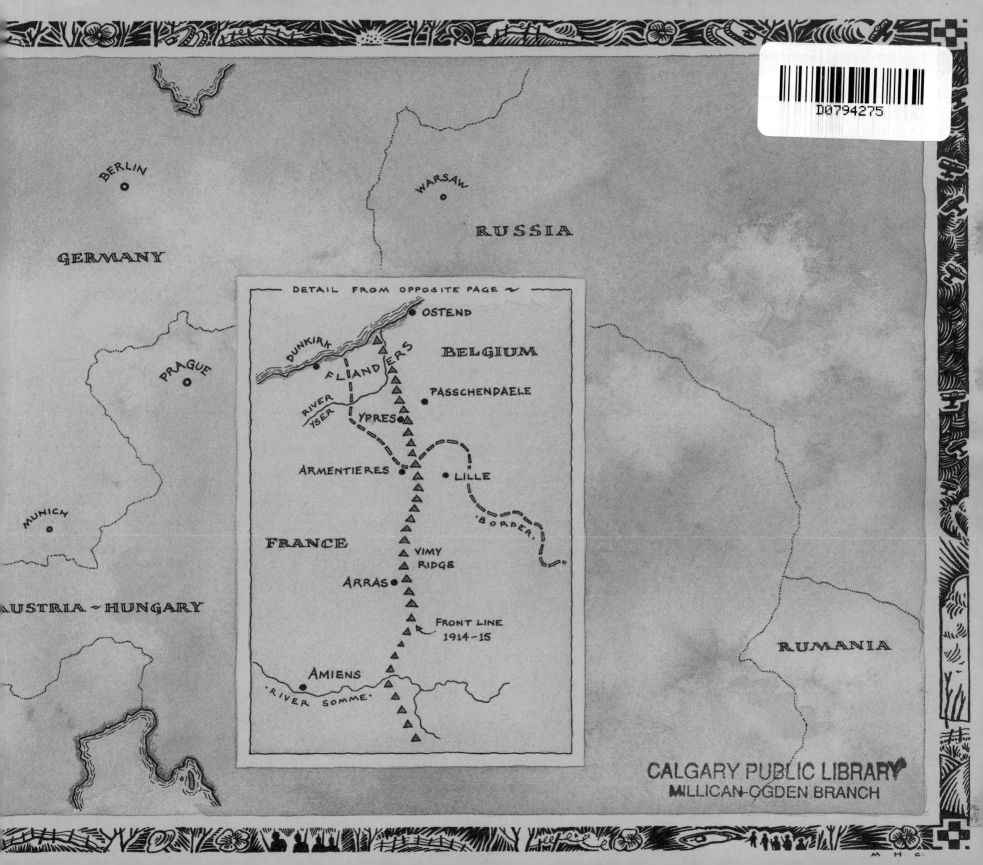

GERMANY

BERLIN
○

WARSAW
○

RUSSIA

PRAGUE
○

MUNICH
○

AUSTRIA ~ HUNGARY

RUMANIA

DETAIL FROM OPPOSITE PAGE ~

OSTEND ●

BELGIUM

DUNKIRK ●

FLANDERS

RIVER YSER

YPRES ●

PASSCHENDAELE ●

ARMENTIERES ●

● LILLE

·BORDER·

FRANCE

VIMY RIDGE

ARRAS ●

FRONT LINE 1914-15

AMIENS ●

·RIVER SOMME·

In
Flanders Fields

The Story of the Poem by John McCrae

Linda Granfield • Illustrated by Janet Wilson

LESTER PUBLISHING

For my family's soldiers

Clarence S. Boyd—U.S. Army/First World War
Joseph J. Granfield—U.S. Air Force/Second World War
Kerry M. Granfield—U.S. Army
Christopher T. Granfield—U.S. Army

— L.G.

In memory of my father, Douglas Reid, 12th Field Regiment, 43rd Battery, Royal Canadian Artillery, Guelph, Ontario, and my grandfather, Tom Wright, who was wounded on Flanders fields.

— J.W.

Text copyright © 1995 by Linda Granfield
Illustrations copyright © 1995 by Janet Wilson

Canadian Cataloguing in Publication Data

Granfield, Linda
In Flanders Fields : the story of the poem by John McCrae

ISBN 1-895555-65-5

1. McCrae, John, 1872–1918. In Flanders fields.
2. World War, 1914–1918 – Literature and the war –
Juvenile literature. I. Wilson, Janet, 1952–   . II. Title.

PS8525.C72I534   1995   C811'.52   C95-930774-5
PR9199.2.M33I534   1995

Acknowledgements

The author and illustrator would like to express their heartfelt gratitude, first and foremost, to Bev Dietrich and Robin Etherington of Guelph Museums (Ontario) for access to the McCrae archives and for their valuable professional assistance. Thanks as well go to Desmond Morton; the staff of Holts' Battlefield Tours Ltd., England; the American Legion; the Royal Canadian Legion; Vetcraft Industries, Toronto; and the Museum of Applied Military History—20th Battalion C. E. F. Kathy Lowinger and Janice Weaver of Lester Publishing, designer Annabelle Stanley, and Cal Smiley and Chris Wilson all deserve special mention for their support and many efforts "behind the lines." And finally, a word of thanks to the numerous historians, biographers, and artists who passionately chronicled the First World War in words and pictures that influenced our text and paintings.

Lester Publishing Limited
56 The Esplanade
Toronto, Ontario
Canada M5E 1A7

Front cover: Janet Wilson
Back cover: National Archives of Canada (PA 2195)
Endpapers: Malcolm Cullen
Design: Annabelle Stanley
Printed and bound in Canada

95 96 97 98 5 4 3 2 1

Picture Credits: p. 10: recruitment poster, courtesy of Guelph Museums: McCrae House; p. 11: John McCrae, courtesy of Guelph Museums: McCrae House; sketch of cadet uniform by Janet Wilson; p. 12: postcard of war-ravaged Ypres, author's collection; p. 13: sketch of soldier with carrier pigeon by Janet Wilson; p. 18: McCrae with horse and dog, courtesy of Guelph Museums: McCrae House; p. 19: Victory Bonds ad, sketch by John McCrae, both courtesy of Guelph Museums: McCrae House; p. 20: sketch of trenches by Janet Wilson; p. 21: battlefields of Passchendaele, courtesy of National Archives of Canada (PA 2195); p. 28: McCrae's funeral, courtesy of Guelph Museums: McCrae House; p. 29: First World War medal, courtesy of Guelph Museums: McCrae House; p. 30: Poppy Day ad, courtesy of Guelph Museums: McCrae House; p. 31: sketch of veteran and child by Janet Wilson; p. 32: first commemorative poppy, courtesy of Guelph Museums: McCrae House.

In Flanders Fields

—

In Flanders fields the poppies blow
Between the crosses, row on row,
That mark our place; and in the sky
The larks, still bravely singing, fly
Scarce heard amid the guns below.

We are the Dead. Short days ago
We lived, felt dawn, saw sunset glow,
Loved, and were loved, and now we lie
          In Flanders fields.

Take up our quarrel with the foe:
To you from failing hands we throw
  The torch; be yours to hold it high.
  If ye break faith with us who die
We shall not sleep, though poppies grow
          In Flanders fields

John McCrae

MAY 1915. IN FLANDERS, the French and Belgian lands bordered by the North Sea, it was the time for fresh green shoots and white blossoms. But the First World War had raged for nearly a year and winter's gloom remained, etched upon the skies by blackened tree trunks, ruined church spires, and barbed wire.

For nearly two weeks John McCrae, a Canadian medical officer, had attended to the horrible injuries suffered by soldiers in the continuing Second Battle of Ypres. While shells exploded around them, McCrae and his staff cared for hundreds of wounded men each day. And others, companions they had shared a meal with just hours before, were buried a few steps from the dressing-station door. "It was HELL all the time," McCrae later wrote. "We really expected to die in our tracks. We never had our boots off, much less our clothes."

On the second dismal day of May, one death in particular touched John McCrae. A close friend, Lieutenant Alexis Helmer, was killed early that morning when an enemy shell exploded at his feet. John McCrae, doctor, could do nothing to save him; but John McCrae, soldier and friend, recited prayers as Helmer's remains were lowered into the Flanders soil and the grave marked with a wooden cross.

Reports concerning the hours after Helmer's burial differ. One states that McCrae sat on the back step of an ambulance, writing within sight of the new grave. Another says the doctor wrote off and on while bandaging the wounded. *What* he was writing, however, proved more important than *where* he wrote it. Helmer's death inspired McCrae to write "In Flanders Fields," a poem that to this day relays the images of war, loss, love, and renewal.

After he completed the poem, John McCrae was back at work in the dressing-station. The war was to continue for three more years . . . in Flanders fields and beyond.

In Flanders fields the poppies blow

Between the crosses, row on row,

That mark our place; and in the sky

The larks, still bravely singing, fly

Scarce heard amid the guns below.

 **WHEN THE FIRST WORLD WAR,** the Great War, began in August 1914, no one knew that millions of young men and women would die before the conflict ended in 1918. No one knew that villages would be erased from the map, or that entire nations would be changed forever. In fact, people thought the war would be over before Christmas.

There was no single reason why the war began. Some European countries, like Germany, craved more power. Others, like France, wanted revenge for past wrongs, and Britain feared Germany's growing fleet and industrial power. People were primed for war. The murder of the heir to the Austro-Hungarian throne, in June 1914, was the spark that lit this ready tinder.

When the German army moved into neutral Belgium, Britain upheld its treaty obligations to defend the Belgians. On August 4, 1914, the British government announced: "War, Germany, act." People danced in the streets. Britain was at war!

But the Great War was unlike any other in history. It was a new and horrible artillery battle fought from rat-infested, water-filled trenches dug deep into foreign soil. There would be little noble about it, except the dedication of millions to fight for what they believed. Into the nightmarish terrain of the Western Front stepped John McCrae.

McCrae's ancestors included soldiers and physicians, and he carried on the tradition. As a boy in Guelph, Ontario, he won a gold medal for being the best drilled cadet in the province. By fifteen he was a bugler in his father's battery, and by eighteen he was a gunner. While in university, McCrae belonged to the Queen's Own Rifles. Medical school was followed by American and Canadian hospital work and teaching. All the while, McCrae wrote short stories and poetry in which peace after death was a repeated theme.

The battlefields of Flanders were not the first John McCrae had ever encountered. In 1900 he sailed from Halifax, Nova Scotia, to South Africa, where the Boer War was blazing. There he saw firsthand the cost of battle, though still he believed that a man must fight evil wherever he encountered it. After a year in South Africa, McCrae returned to Canada, and for ten years he was a doctor and a teacher, not a soldier.

McCrae was in England on holiday when war was declared in 1914, yet he answered Canada's call for recruits. "I'm available as a combatant or medical if they need me," he cabled home.

But after a year in Flanders, McCrae wrote to a close friend, "I saw enough fighting to do me for my natural life." Millions of other men from many nations no doubt agreed.

John McCrae

Highland cadet corps uniform

YPRES, A FOURTEENTH-CENTURY town encircled by a moat, had been the home of a beautiful medieval cathedral and Cloth Hall. By the time John McCrae arrived in Flanders, however, the town, called "Wipers" by the soldiers, was ruined and refugees streamed from it. Troops were camped not far from the Yser Canal, where they cooked meals, wrote letters to loved ones, and strengthened friendships that, in some instances, began back in their homeland.

A soldier's day included a great deal of waiting: waiting in line for a once-a-week (or month) shower; waiting for dark to fall so the wounded could be removed from the battle-field; waiting to be seen by a nurse or a doctor; waiting for food and water, and perhaps going for days without either one.

When a soldier wasn't fighting, there were chores to be done. Trench-digging and covering the muck with duckboards, a kind of wooden boardwalk, took up much of the time. Communication lines, trucks, rifles, and even cooking utensils needed repair. The pigeons that carried vital messages had to be exercised. Rations had to be transported and the mail had to be delivered. (One soldier wrote of a "week's accumulation . . . 165 bags.") There were drill parades and training sessions.

Many off-duty hours were spent "chat-ting," removing chats (lice) from the seams of clothing. Such tasks gave a soldier time to gossip with his comrades and learn more

YPRES AFTER TWO YEARS OF WAR.　　Nº9

about where they came from, whom they loved, and what they would do when the war was over. Emotional ties grew. In the trenches, soldiers fought as much for the protection of the fellow next to them as for any other, more patriotic, reason.

The soldiers' meals were a monotonous menu of canned stew, pork and beans, and "bully" (corned) beef. Three men might share one loaf of fresh or mouldy bread, with tinned fruit for dessert. A mug of hot tea was a welcome source of heat during the winter months. (Some soldiers even shaved with cold tea when there were fresh water shortages.) Time spent at rest, away from the trenches, meant a man could enjoy treats like bacon and eggs in a nearby cottage, or at an *estaminet* (canteen) in the village.

Packages received from home were filled with necessities like soap and handmade socks, but also gave the soldiers something they could share: cookies, peppermint drops, cocoa, raisins, and almonds. Such luxuries provided brief moments of pleasure in an otherwise grimy and depressing situation.

Long after the war, many veterans still recalled the daily terrors, but also relished sharing happier memories: lighthearted sing-alongs (several songs performed with new, rude verses), or ball games played within earshot of the fighting. Some soldiers joined army bands. One group even held a military circus, complete with equestrian contests and a Grand Circus Parade. Drinking, smoking, card-playing, and visits to town provided much needed relief from the ever present horrors.

We are the Dead. Short days ago

We lived, felt dawn, saw sunset glow,

Loved, and were loved,

and now we lie / In Flanders fields.

SOON AFTER HE WROTE "In Flanders Fields," John McCrae sent the poem to England for possible publication. It appeared, without his name, in the December 8, 1915, issue of *Punch* magazine. The public response was overwhelming. The poet's identity was subsequently revealed, and his work became known as "the most popular English poem of the Great War." People recited, translated, and "answered" McCrae's poem. "In Flanders Fields" was particularly well-received in the United States, a country not yet involved in the conflict. In just fifteen lines, McCrae had captured the mood of the times.

Although, as a doctor, McCrae was committed to saving lives, he was equally committed to the war effort. "It is a terrible state of affairs," he wrote, "and I am going [to war] because I think every bachelor, especially if he has experience of war, ought to go. I am really rather afraid, but more afraid to stay at home with my conscience . . ." At forty-one, McCrae was too old and unpractised to command an artillery brigade as he wished, but he was named brigade-surgeon.

❖

During the war, John McCrae found comfort, joy, and time for reflection while riding his horse, Bonfire, and playing with his faithful dog, Bonneau.

The publication of "In Flanders Fields" enabled McCrae to help the cause more than he had ever imagined. Men inspired by the final stanza's call-to-arms joined the army when it most needed new recruits. In 1917 the first Victory Loan Bonds in Canada used lines from the poem in their advertisements. The bonds raised the spectacular sum of $400 million for the war effort. John McCrae was pleased by such news.

"If ye break faith — we shall not sleep"

BUY VICTORY BONDS

Throughout his adolescence and university years, McCrae had artistically arranged hundreds of tickets, magazine illustrations, and photographs in a colourful scrapbook. On one page, he pasted pictures of famous poets and copied the lines "They are slaves who will not dare / All wrongs to right, all rights to share." Twenty years later, John McCrae was doing his best to right wrongs, and he urged the world's citizens to join him.

Sketch of the **Laurentian** *by John McCrae.*

TRENCHES WERE ZIGZAGGING alleys carved deep into the soil and sandbagged for support and protection. Soldiers moved through a three-line system of trenches: the outlying reserve trench; the support trench; and then the fire trench, which looked across "no man's land," a shell-scarred area that separated the soldiers' trenches from the enemy's. Fierce-looking loops of barbed wire stretched endlessly along the front of the fire trench.

In bad weather, rain filled the trenches. Days of standing in the cold, stagnant water left men with a dangerous condition called trench foot, which is similar to frostbite. Rats and brutal winter weather added to the misery. Soldiers slept in "funk holes" (shelves scraped into the sides of the trench). There were latrines and two-man listening posts where soldiers monitored the enemy's movements. Many soldiers' letters described the sound of bullets cracking around them as they sat in the dark, waiting.

Combat could take place at any time of the day or night, and often continued for several days straight. Even when the fighting eased, every soldier was required to "stand to," fully dressed and ready for action, for an hour at dawn and dusk each day. When the enemy did

Mud holes in the battlefields of Passchendaele, November 1917.

approach, or it was time for an Allied attack, the gunners manned their artillery and the infantry prepared to "go over the top" (a phrase used to describe the practice of leaping out of the deep trenches into no man's land).

Snipers and heavy artillery fire, as well as poisonous gas attacks, provided the military doctors with thousands of patients. Bronchitis, pneumonia, and influenza spread quickly among soldiers in such close, unhealthy quarters. War wounds often had to be treated on the field by a soldier's comrades, rather than a doctor, so each soldier carried a bit of iodine and some bandages in his pocket. After dark, a stretcher squad of four men would lift the wounded to their shoulders and stumble across the bomb-scarred field, all the while dodging snipers' bullets and mud holes that could claim them.

At the dressing-station, doctors and nurses treated those with minor injuries and determined which of the seriously wounded soldiers would be sent to better-equipped hospitals in France, or to England for major rehabilitation. Once he was back on his feet, a soldier who had spent a few weeks in a soft hospital bed in England would find himself in the muddy trenches again, replacing yet another wounded comrade.

Take up our quarrel with the foe:

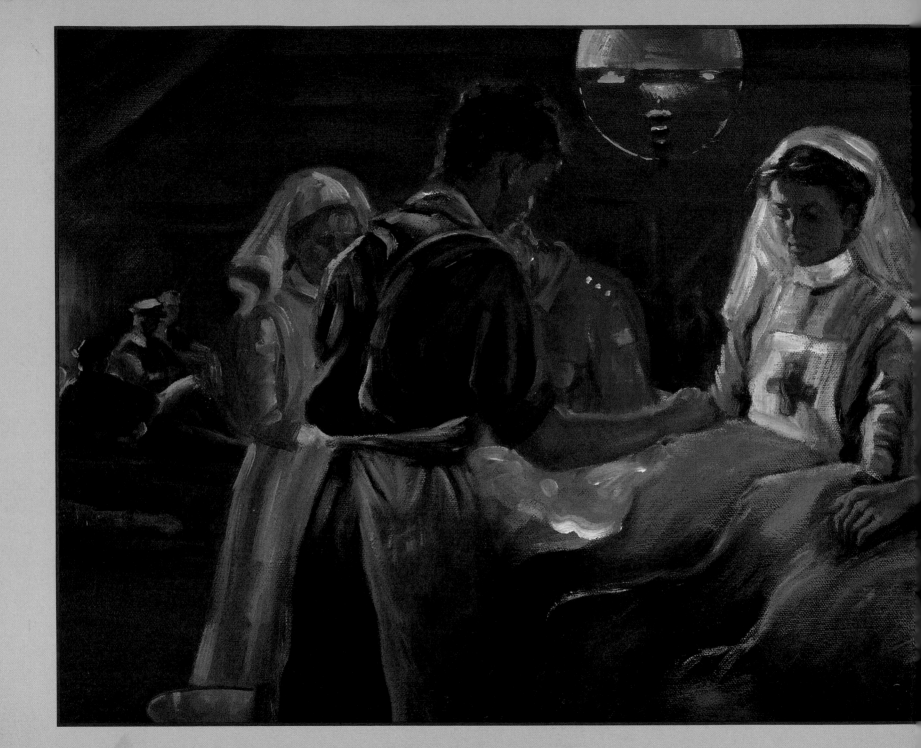

To you from failing hands we throw

The torch; be yours to hold it high.

JOHN MCCRAE TREATED INJURED soldiers in dressing-stations, tent hospitals, and buildings so cold there was frost on the floor. He handled the survivors of some of the war's most devastating battles: Second Ypres, the Somme, Vimy Ridge, and Passchendaele. People who knew McCrae noticed changes in his appearance and personality. He spent more time alone and looked older than he actually was. He no longer entertained companions with lively stories, told with a winning smile. "I am very tired of it," he wrote to a friend. No wonder. His hospital treated nearly five thousand men in the first half of July 1916, and almost seven hundred on the twenty-first of July alone.

John McCrae was demoralized and unhealthy by the winter of 1918. Ill in bed, he learned of his appointment as consulting physician to the First British Army. Within a week of the announcement, on the twenty-eighth of January, McCrae died of pneumonia and meningitis. The sun shone brightly as John McCrae, doctor, soldier, and poet, was buried with full military honours in the cemetery at Wimereux, France.

News of McCrae's death spread quickly around the world. His elderly father, David McCrae, began to paste hundreds of tributes into his own scrapbook. Like so many other lost sons, John McCrae would sleep forever where the poppies grow. But even in death, his voice, through his famous poem, continued to call on citizens to support a war that was nearing its end at last.

John McCrae's funeral in 1918.

THE UNITED STATES JOINED the Allies in 1917, and the fighting continued. Countries were ruined, and people and resources were exhausted. Some officials thought the war might go on until 1920, but improved tanks, airplanes, and renewed military strategies brought it to a gradual end. In the early morning hours of November 11, 1918, the Armistice, an agreement to end the fighting, was signed. By the eleventh hour of the eleventh day of the eleventh month, after nearly sixteen hundred days of war, the guns were silenced.

Millions had been killed and thousands more returned home with permanently damaged bodies. Still others admitted they were "wounded in [their] minds." For some families, a lifetime of searching for missing loved ones began. Few people were left untouched by the horrors of the battlefield.

Memorials began to dot the countrysides of many nations, "lest we forget." Every November 11 at eleven a.m., silence descends on streets everywhere as millions of people pause to reflect on the enormous losses sustained by the world during wartime. To this day, "In Flanders Fields" is recited during remembrance ceremonies around the world.

Some people argue that the poem's invitation to battle is unsettling, while others recognize it as an expression of John McCrae's personal beliefs and an example of social attitudes of the time. While most everyone can agree that war has never erased the problems of the world, we continue to honour the memory of those who sacrificed themselves for a cause they believed to be great and just. Often, voices of peace, like McCrae's larks, may *scarce* be heard, but they *can* be heard . . . if only we will listen.

If ye break faith with us who die

We shall not sleep, though poppies grow / In Flanders fields.

THROUGHOUT HISTORY, THE SCARLET corn poppy has been a symbol of life. But after the publication of "In Flanders Fields" in 1915, it became a universal symbol of remembrance. The sturdy flower blossomed on the makeshift graves that were hastily dug during the war and, on the bombarded landscape of western Europe, seemed to thrive where nothing else could. Soldiers often picked the bright flowers and wore them on their helmets.

During the war, posters promoted wearing poppies in honour of the war dead. In 1919 a group of Americans, welcoming troops home, stripped the poppy decorations from a refreshment booth and left donations behind. Veterans' organizations soon realized that the demand for poppies could benefit disabled soldiers and families left in need by the war. The British and American Legions adopted the poppy as their memorial flower. By 1921 silk

poppies made by French war widows and orphans were among the first remembrance flowers sold in North America. Meanwhile, in Europe, the long process of reburying the war dead began. Soldiers' remains were moved from the battlefields to military cemeteries, and the crude wooden crosses were replaced by rows of neat stone markers.

"Poppy mania" continued through the 1920s, and communities were urged to plant family and town poppy gardens. In Canada, John McCrae's homeland, there was even some talk of replacing the national symbol, the maple leaf, with a scarlet poppy.

Each year millions of poppies, reminders of the soldiers of the First World War and every conflict since then, are constructed of silk, plastic, paper, or felt. They are still handmade, and are sold by veterans and volunteers around the world. The funds collected are recycled into programs for veterans and their families.

The scarlet blooms we wear on our lapels today represent remembrance and life, just like the sturdy poppies that still blossom in the once-bloody fields of Flanders.

A French veteran receives a poppy.

Lest We Forget